RULES for
HUSBANDS

RULES FOR HUSBANDS

James Dale and Ellen Small

**Andrews McMeel
Publishing**

Kansas City

01 02 03 04 05 BRG 10 9 8 7 6 5 4 3 2 1

Library of Congress Cataloging-in-Publication Data

Dale, Jim, 1948–
    Rules for husbands / James Dale and Ellen Small.
        p. cm.
    ISBN 0-7407-1884-3
    1. Husbands—Miscellanea. 2. Marriage—Miscellanea. 3. Wives—Psychology—Miscellanea. I. Small, Ellen. II. Title.
HQ756 .D37 2001
306.872—dc21   2001046407

Book design by Holly Camerlinck

attention: SCHOOLS and BUSINESSES

Andrews McMeel books are available at quantity discounts with bulk purchase for educational, business, or sales promotional use. For information, please write to: Special Sales Department, Andrews McMeel Publishing, 4520 Main Street, Kansas City, Missouri 64111.

Rules for Husbands

IntRoDuCtion

Here they are, the rules you've been waiting for. The rules you didn't even know existed. The rules no one told you about when you went on a date that led to a date that led to a ring.

Your own father never sat you down and said, "Son, in marriage, sometimes you have to give up the remote control." Your married buddies never took you aside and said, "Every once in a while, buy flowers." Your old roommate never advised you, "'Bubba' isn't a romantic nickname for your wife."

Nobody ever said there were rules or guidelines or laws you'd need in order to deal with the opposite sex.

You thought this husband-wife stuff came naturally.

Wrong! There's nothing natural about it. Why do you think they call them the "opposite" sex? They're a species unto themselves.

You have to know the rules. If you want a driver's license, you have to know the laws. (Same goes for hunting and fishing.) And just like driving, in marriage, if you do something wrong, you get a ticket.

Being a terminal slob is punishable by a fine of heavy glaring and up to three days of one-syllable communication. Forgetting an anniversary is the DUI of marriage. You will serve time in solitary and have to attend a treatment program.

But now, screened, tested, and proven by thousands of veteran husbands who followed (and husbands who ignored) these immutable laws, written down in one handy guidebook, are: the *Rules for Husbands*.

If you follow these rules, will you have a perfect marriage? Who knows? What is a perfect marriage, anyway? Yours, mine, or someone else's?

But one thing is certain: If you flagrantly disregard these rules, you will have a mad wife. In which case, see Rule One: Apologize.

apologize

You don't think you've done anything wrong, so why apologize? Because you have done something wrong, you just don't know what it is yet. Apologize and be ahead of the game.

THe Remote Control is Not your Manhood

You love the power. That long, smooth, slim, potent, magical device in your hand. Point it and images change in front of your eyes. Click it and you determine the fate of every show. The Shopping Network? No way. *Fashion Emergency?* Forget it. *Oprah?* No, no, no. CNN? Only during a war. *The Simpsons?* Okay. *Law and Order* reruns? Hmm. ESPN? Yes, yes, yes!!

But marriage is about sharing. And that means sometimes letting her hold the remote . . . and pointing it and clicking . . . and yes, deciding what you watch, even if it's one of those movies on the Lifetime Network.

Pay attention

Or at least look like you're paying attention.*

* See "Really Listen" on page 22.

an aPPLianCE
IS Not a GIft

a blender, toaster, food processor, waffle iron, pasta machine, or bread maker—no matter how cool, how French, how state-of-the-art, even if endorsed by Wolfgang Puck, Emeril Lagasse, and Martha Stewart—is still a machine to make food that you will probably eat. An appliance is not a gift; it's a tool. You like tools. She likes gifts.

BeWaRe of MinefieLDS

Never answer the question, "Do you think I've gained weight?" unless you have a death wish.

SOMETIMES SHE DOESN'T REALLY WANT YOUR OPINION

When your wife asks one of the following:

How do I look?

How does this dress look?

How does my hair look?

How do these shoes look with this outfit?

How does my butt look in these pants?

She is *not* really asking you a question. She does not want an honest assessment, an evaluation, or any suggestions. She is asking if you love her.

Answer any and all questions that contain the word "look" with the response, "Great!" It's the only good response and it's only good if delivered fast and emphatically. Do not hesitate. Hesitation suggests doubt; doubt suggests perhaps someone else looks better; and you're just having an affair in your mind, aren't you, you slimy lizard?!

act Knightly Daily

You don't have to slay dragons. Just open the door for her now and then. Walk her to the car. Pay the check. Drop her near the door if it's raining. Why? Because it's nice. Outdated, old-fashioned, rare, out of sync with modern society, but nice. Nice does not go out of style.

Let Her See your
Power Tools

Now this is a chance to display your true manliness. Show her your cordless screwdriver. Your four-speed drill. Your grinder. Your chain saw.

Do a demo. Turn them on. "Rip" a piece of lumber. "Bore" a hole through an actual piece of wood. Put another piece of wood behind it. Insert a screw and "fasten" the two boards together! She will be awed.

Don't let her touch your tools.

BARBECUE

You are, after all, a man.

There you are, Homo sapien, standing in front of a blazing inferno (charcoal or propane), beer in one hand, fork with built-in thermometer in the other, able to transform a mere piece of cow flesh into a slice of sirloin heaven.

All you need is the $5,000 tempered steel, mahogany-trimmed, brushed chrome, electro-start, double-domed, triple rack, surround-a-flame, accu-temp, Mercedes Turbo Grill.

Man! Meat! Fire! Good!

Don't Be a Cliché.
Be Bob.

Okay, so you barbecue. That's nice, but the occasional steak and corn-on-the-cob-cooked-in-foil-under-the-coals is not a major contribution to the marriage deal.

Don't be another guy who can't or won't cook indoors in that room called the kitchen. Learn to make something. Anything. Meatloaf. Make it your dish: Bob's Meatloaf. Then add variations: Bob's Meatloaf with Bob's Potatoes. Bob's Meatloaf Subs. Bob's Meatloaf Omelets. Bob's Meatloaf Surprise (something inside Bob's Meatloaf). Bob's Meatloaf Soup (pieces of Bob's Meatloaf in Bob's hot water). Robert's Meatloaf (Bob's Meatloaf made with ground sirloin instead of ground chuck). Bob's Leftover Meatloaf (self-explanatory).

As your confidence grows, spread your wings, so to speak. Bob's Chicken Wings. Bob's Thighs. Bob's Breasts. Bob's Whole Barbecue Chicken! Move on to pasta. Bob's

Special Tortellini (toss in some of that chicken). Now try seafood. Bob's Tuna. Bob's Fish Sticks. Bob's Shrimp (whoa!). Pretty soon you'll have a whole menu. And you can bring back old favorites like Bob's Meatloaf.

Just take responsibility for some of the meals some of the time. It isn't the culinary quality, it's the domestic effort. And it's not expecting someone else (her) to do it.

If you really can't cook, provide. Pick up. Order out. Drive-through. Meals do not appear on tables. Someone puts them there. It could be you, Bob.

Wait Patiently

The two of you are going out for the evening. You need two minutes and fourteen seconds to kick off your sneakers, put on "good shoes," spray your armpits, and pull a semiclean shirt over your head.

She has more to do than you. Things you can't even imagine. Rituals of beauty. Rituals take time.

If you can't actually be patient, pretend. Or find something to do, like your income taxes for next year. Don't tap your watch. Don't pace. Don't help by handing her the eyeliner thing. Just accept the fact that she'll take much longer than you. She'll look much better than you.

SHOWER REGULARLY

You're a man. You stink.

Don't Leave a Clothing Trail

Do not undress by dropping your clothing, one item at a time, across the floor, from jacket to sweater to shirt to pants to underwear to shoes to socks. You are not Hansel leaving a trail home for Gretel. You're a pig. Pick up your stuff.

Read and Follow Instructions

You know those little printed, folded over, twelve-to-eight-hundred-page, written-in-Spanish, Japanese, Norwegian, and bad English booklets with letters, numbers, arrows, and purposely unclear drawings of wall A, wall B, wall C, leg A, leg C *(where is leg B?)*, pegs 1 through 134, tabs fitting into slots, grooves receiving groovettes, and assorted grommets, bolts, nuts, hooks, and hookettes? You know, the booklets that are sealed in the plastic bag, buried under a cubic mile of Styrofoam peanuts inside those massive corrugated, reinforced, double-thick cardboard, glued, lashed, and stapled, impossible-to-open containers that contain things like picnic tables, computers, stereos, bookshelves, hanging bird feeders, car bike racks, air conditioners, humidifiers, dehumidifiers, rehumidifiers, spice racks, bike racks, barbecue grills, and swing-seesaw-sandbox play sets? You know, *those* instructions?

Do not throw them away. Do not ignore them. Do not assume "any fool can put an outdoor shed together." Do not spend an entire Saturday cursing the #%!!**@! missing flange caplette. (What *is* a flange caplette?) In other words, do not be a man.

The instructions are there for a reason. To instruct. Read and follow. You will not be drummed out of the husband's union. You will be able to stand back and say, "I built that outdoor hammock. Well, at least I stretched the netted thing over the hooky things."

ask DiRections

You're lost. Admit it. Will you get to wherever you're going without asking directions? Maybe. Eventually. But eventually is a long time. Ask someone how to get there. Get there before eventually. And no part of your anatomy will get smaller. Promise.

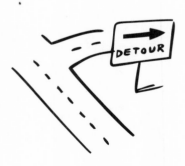

TRY THE HIGH-tech APPROACH TO BEING Late: CALL

That way she won't assume a) you're dead on the highway or b) you're doing something you're not supposed to be doing and as good as dead on the highway.

Stay Awake

Go to one musical, opera, ballet, or symphony this year. Somehow, keep your eyes open through the whole thing. Even if you hate musicals, opera, ballet, and/or symphonies. Going—and staying awake—shows you are willing to put your own wishes second sometimes. Think of the things she's endured for you.

Besides, a little culture won't hurt you. (A lot of culture, however, might crowd some key sports statistics out of your brain.)

stay awake after . . .

Making love. Speak. Hold her. Then you can fall into a deathlike coma.

Really Listen

It's more than head nodding. It's not just waiting for your turn to talk. It's hearing what she says (or doesn't say) and getting it.

Do not risk failing the "If you were really listening, then what did I just say?" test.

Remember Key Dates

Men are notorious for not remembering critical dates in their relationships. Her birthday; your anniversary; when you got engaged; the day your friend called to suggest you call to ask her out; the date, day of the week, place, and exact time of your first date; your second, third, fourth, and fifth dates; the one year anniversary of your first date; the five-year anniversary of your fifth date . . .

These are what memories are made of. If you don't remember them, you obviously don't care. If you don't care . . . well, you don't even want to go there.

There's only one way to remember all these dates—the same way you memorized those dates in junior high school history:

1066—The Battle of Hastings

1215—Magna Carta

1492—Columbus discovered America

Write them on your palm.

engage In Retail Meandering

Go shopping with your wife. Yes, even when you don't need anything. Just go and look at things. It's a good way to spend time together. Granted, you can't keep score, root for the home team, or bet on shopping. But it's better than many other activities, e.g. picking out wallpaper.

Don't Count Her Shoes

The number of pairs of shoes she has will never make sense to you. Logic says no one needs more than two, maybe three, pairs of shoes.

Why so many kinds of sandals? Why thongs, roped, flip-flop, ergonomic, and painful? Why high heels of every height by 1/8 inch increments? Why pointy toes, square toes, round toes, and no toes? Same goes for straps? And why all those colors? Is there really a need for peach shoes? How about turquoise? What's the difference between bright white, off-white, milky white, starch white, eggshell, ecru, sand, salt, and powdered sugar white? And don't even get started on the varieties of black.

Forget it. There is no rational, sensible, reasonable explanation for having so many pairs of shoes. Wives just aren't as logical as husbands.

By, the way, why do you need so many cable channels?

avoiD tHe "Man" eXcuse

Don't use it. "I'm a man so I can't (fill in any task),"
e.g. give birth, attend a bridal shower, breast-feed. Okay,
technically, there are some things you cannot do or should
not attempt. But you can be there at the birth, pick up a gift
for the shower, and get up at three A.M. to sit with your wife
while she breast-feeds. Or you can do night bottle feedings.
Turn on the TV. ESPN is on twenty-four hours a day. Catch
up on Indonesian soccer scores.

The idea isn't to do the anatomically impossible, but to
do more of the husbandly possible.

eXPLaiN FiSHiNG aND/OR GOLF

explain fishing: Why you like standing in cold water. (It feels good and no one is bothering me.) The value of silence. (It's so quiet.) Fooling a scaly creature with a miniature brain. (It's cool.) If you explain it well, she'll never want to go.

If you don't fish, explain golf: Why you swing a long stick at a little ball. (Obviously, to see if I can keep it from getting lost in the woods.) How come you get so mad if you're having fun. (I wasn't mad. I was concentrating loud.)

Same idea, different addiction.

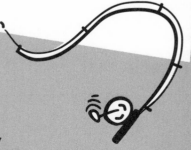

Get in TOUCH WiTH yOUR Feminine SiDe (OR, at Least, Get in TOUCH WiTH HeRS): BUy FLOWeRS

You don't even like walking into a flower shop. How do you pick out something you don't know the names of? (Is there a difference between an iris and a lilac?) How come one kind of flower costs more than another? Why do all of them cost so much? They're just colored heads on the end of green sticks. Why do you have to get a dozen? Why not just one really nice one? Why do they cut off the ends? What's that other green leafy thing they put in with them? And what's with the card? You hate having to write something on the card. And you have to do it in front of someone else. (Or

28

worse, if you call in the order, you have to tell some stranger who's snickering at you what to put on the card.) Why do you have to do this flower stuff?

Why? Because someone else may like flowers. Your wife. Don't be such a guy.

SHARING

Sharing household jobs is not taking the garbage out and expecting a "thank you."

Get off the Bench

Don't think you're doing a favor when you wash the dishes, dry the dishes, vacuum, push the little red button on the washing machine, throw your underwear in the hamper, put a towel back after using it, replace the toilet paper when it's out, unload the groceries, turn on the disposal, change a lightbulb, throw out milk that's six weeks past its expiration date, dust, wipe, straighten, or fold.

These things are called life. You're a player, not a spectator. Don't just watch and applaud.

TURN THINGS OFF

Interestingly, household devices do not generally turn themselves off. Light switches, sinks, showers, TVs, stereos, ovens, toasters, coffeepots. Men turn them on but rarely turn them off. But then, the next day, men turn them on again. How do you think they got turned off?

Magic?

or

Your wife?

Pick one. No, guess again. Right.

Next time, try turning to *off*. It isn't hard. It's just *on* in reverse.

Put Things away

Same as the *on-off* theory. Things—like socks, pants, bread, ice cream containers, cereal boxes, dishes, glasses, forks, spoons, books, games, CDs, magazines, shoes, towels, toothpaste—don't put themselves back into the cupboard/closet/package/drawer/medicine cabinet/refrigerator when we stop using them. They just sit there. (They're so lazy.) But somehow, they're back in the cupboard the next day. Guess how? No, not elves.

Next time, try it. Take out, put back. Take out, put back. See, it's not that hard. Even a guy can do it.

Get out of touch with your inner slob.

DO tHE DiSHeS

Why? Because they're dirty, Einstein.

BeWaRe TemPoRaRY DoMesTiC BLiNDNesS

You say, "Honey, where's the ice cream?" Do you really wonder where it is? Have you lost it? Does no logical location for something called "ice cream" immediately come to mind? Or are you just finding a squirrely way to say, "Would you get me some ice cream?"

The ice cream is in the freezer. You know that. Otherwise it would soon be Rocky Road milk. Get it yourself.

By the way, the toilet paper is in the hall cupboard. The aspirin is in the medicine cabinet. And that nice, warm down comforter (when you don't want to get out of bed on a cold night) is in the linen closet.

TURN tHe FaN "ON" (REMEMBER? OPPOSitE Of "OFF")

You may be very proud of what you do in there. But, now that you're an adult and potty trained, no one else wants to know about it. Certainly not your wife. So turn on the fan. Take advantage of the exhaust and the noise camouflage. One more thing: Flush.

Toilet Seat? Down (This Is Pretty Basic Stuff)

You don't think it's such a big deal to leave the seat up? Try this. Lift the lid and the seat. Take your pants down. Sit on the porcelain. Cool and refreshing? No, ice-cold and painful. Now try doing it in the dark, at three A.M.

DO NOT BURP AND THEN GIGGLE

Only men (and their sons) think burping is funny.

THe caSTRo RULe

Smoke cigars outside. Better yet, in Cuba.

Be Prepared to Sacrifice a Friend to the God of Marriage

You want your friends to be her friends and her friends to be your friends and everybody to be everybody's friend. And, generally, it will work.

But there will be someone you care about but who just rubs your wife the wrong way. It might be the guy who taught you how to make that noise with your armpit in the fourth grade and still makes the same noise today. Or the "funniest guy in the whole world" who she thinks is crude, juvenile, and possibly mentally unstable. Or your high school buddy who winks every time he tells an old story about you. Or your old neighbor who only stops by at dinnertime. Or maybe the rich guy with the fancy car, gold watch, and expensive hair who asks what tax bracket you're in. Or your college roommate who is still hitchhiking around the world. Or that middle-aged fellow from your office who dates no one over nineteen.

There will be someone she just doesn't love like you do. She'll try. But eventually your old friend will be her new enemy. He'll get on her nerves. Or under her skin. Or within a mile of your home once too often. And she'll have the overwhelming urge to kill him.

That's when you have to reevaluate. Your friend or your wife? Chances are, he's not quite as great as you might have thought back in the fourth grade or that night you shared NBA draft theories at the sports bar. Maybe he isn't your best friend. Maybe he isn't even in the top ten. Maybe you shouldn't ask him over to the house or see him as often . . . or ever. Maybe he is a psychopath.

Besides, there will be a friend of your wife's who you'll want to trade-off for one of yours. *We won't see my burned-out hitchhiker friend if we don't have to see the witch with too many face-lifts.*

Sometimes you just have to throw a friend on the burning altar of marriage.

KiLL Insects

This may seem like a sexist division of duties. It is. Don't analyze it. Just do it. Generally, men don't mind swatting, spraying, smashing, stepping on, trapping, or poisoning bugs or other rodents. It's the one time when being heartless and unfeeling will be to your advantage.

CHANGE DIAPERS

Stop complaining. You're a grown man. Get over it. If you can stick a hook through a slimy worm, you can wipe up a little ca-ca. (Plus, it's three to one it'll just be pee.)

Don't Touch the Thermostat

Most women are colder than most men, most of the time. They like to set the thermostat between 82 and 106 degrees and sleep under a down comforter.

Then, one day, women reach menopause and are suddenly 40 to 90 degrees hotter than men. They want central air conditioning, window units, overhead fans and blocks of ice in each room, and they set the temperature in single digits.

What do you do? Nothing. Just live with it. Perspire for the first twenty years of marriage. Then, during the big change, get a sweater or Nordic parka.

No matter how hot or cold you are, do not touch that little lever on the thermostat. Do not make the red line go up or down.

Is this fair? No. Who said marriage was fair?

Note: If desperate, stick your head in the freezer or rub your hands over the oven for a few minutes.

Some THiNGS DoN't NeeD FiXiNG

When faced with the problems of life, men and women take entirely different approaches.

Male approach: *Problem? Fix!*

Female approach: *Problem? It'll probably work itself out if I just give myself time to think it over and maybe talk to someone else about it.*

When your wife has a problem, she doesn't necessarily want you, or anyone else, to fix it. She may want you to acknowledge it. Understand it (and her) as she deals with it. Listen to her. Talk if asked.

Let's say her boss's brilliant new ideas are driving her crazy. This does not mean you should a) construct a logical analysis that demonstrates to the boss that his ideas are inherently flawed or b) devise a ten-point plan for getting him fired. Her best friend forgot her birthday. Do not call, e-mail, or even frown at the friend. Your wife hates her new haircut. Put down those scissors!

She wants you to agree that her boss is a jerk; assure her that her best friend is still her best friend; lie and tell her that her haircut looks good.

Don't fix anything. Nothing is broken.

OWn one GooD Suit

every husband should own one good suit. Get your wife to pick it out. You'll look good. For weddings, funerals, job interviews, the really serious stuff. Here's the best part: No matter what you do for a living, you only need one. Just get a few neckties. Better yet, get your wife to pick them out so they actually match your suit.

MaKe a GooD LiViNG

This isn't a male-female thing. It's a practical thing. Contrary to the old cliché, money is not the root of all evil. It is the root of all purchases. And some purchases help make life good. Like food, clothing, a home, transportation, vacations, designer shoes, and cable TV.

So, given a choice, make more money rather than less. Both of you, if possible, but at least one of you. Money, or the lack of, is the top subject couples argue about. They rarely argue about having too much.

So make some money. Get some things. Have a good life.

Do Not Make Fun of OPRAH

She can buy and sell you.

always Be OLDeR THan youR Wife

It's not polite to be younger than your wife. You can be older. You can even be the same age. But you should not be younger. It's just rude.

What if, you ask, you are *not* older than your wife? What do you do if you are, in fact, younger? What a stupid question! Make up a number that is higher than hers. Was that so hard?

NeVeR WeiGH LeSS THaN yOUR Wife

Doctors say being overweight is a threat to your health. Not as much as being thinner than your wife.

Don't Spend More on a Haircut Than She Does

You probably have less than two inches of hair. Yours is a little hair hat on the top of your head. From time to time, it needs trimming. Like the lawn.

She has a lot of hair. Hers can be shaped, waved, permed, curled, dyed, streaked, tipped, highlighted, clipped, snipped, chopped, buzzed, layered, blown, poofed, puffed, or moussed like Meg, Jennifer, Sandra, or Julia.

Your hair will look the same no matter how much or how little you spend. She will always think yours looks good and hers looks bad.

So don't waste your money. Let her waste it on hers.

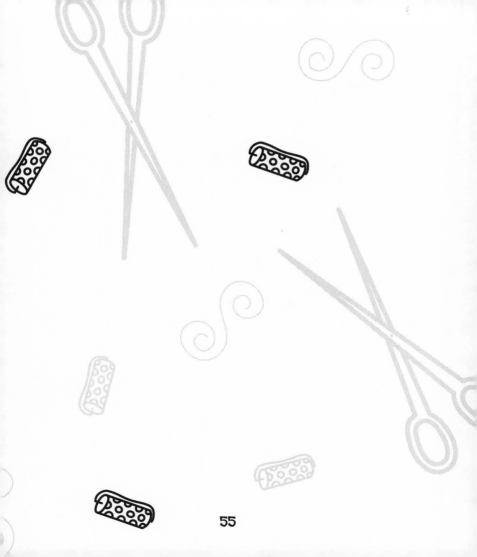

Remember Your Old Girlfriend?

Okay, now forget her. Your wife doesn't want to know about her, see her, meet her, hear about her, or even be aware she exists. Sure, your wife might smile and pretend to be interested, but she actually hates your old girlfriend.

You don't believe it? Okay. Think of it this way: Your wife has an old boyfriend. Do you want to meet him, hang out together, laugh at his jokes, see how handsome he is, how successful he's become . . . Had enough?

a WORD aBOUT FLIRTING: DON'T

Sometimes it's tempting. It might make you feel young and virile for a moment or two.

But is it worth it? Your wife *will* know. And you *will* suffer. Remember those old war movies where the soldier gets caught trying to escape from prison camp and gets put in the solitary, dirty, rat-infested "hole" for a month? Your sentence will be worse.

So if you get the urge to flirt, rent an old war movie instead.

Remember Why
you Fell In Love

every once in a while, when you get aggravated, annoyed, irritated, upset, tired, bored, or testy with each other, stop. Step back. Close your eyes. Remember the woman you fell in love with. How you couldn't resist. You had no control. She was it. You were hooked.

That same woman is in the other room. You married her. She's waiting for you.

Don't TRy to CHange youR Wife

She's a person, not a thing. Don't try to make her a little more this or a little less that. Appreciate her for what she is. Human. In love with you. Emotional. Unpredictable. Real.

She's perfect in her imperfection. Like you.

Be Spontaneous . . .
at Least Quarterly

Surprise her with little things: Dinner. A gift. A card. From out of nowhere. Just because you happened to think of her. Be spur-of-the-moment. And to make sure, put it in your Palm Pilot or Day Runner or tattoo it on your inner thigh.

Do Something Intellectual, Like Going to a Museum

Show your wife that you're thoughtful, sensitive, artistic, and culturally appreciative by suggesting the two of you spend the afternoon at a museum. The Baseball Hall of Fame doesn't count.

Be a Secret Romantic, you Big Slug

Shut up and stop complaining! You can do it when there's no one else around. Watch a corny movie. Sit on the porch and look at stars. Or rub her feet. (Not to be too crass, but these do pay handsome dividends, if you catch the drift.)

HOLD HANDS

No one should have to tell you to do this. It feels good for both of you.

Master the Proper Use of Nicknames

Call her by a romantic name like Honey-Bunny or Sweetie. Not Dude or Bubba. She's your wife, not your fraternity brother.

Don't Get Out-Gifted

No matter what you celebrate—Christmas, Hanukkah, Kwanza, birthdays, anniversaries, Valentine's Day, Sweetest Day, Labor Day (always hard to find the right present)—celebrate with equality. Do not over-gift or under-gift. It will make one of you, or maybe both of you, feel bad.

You don't want to get an imported cashmere sweater and give an apron. (On second thought, never give an apron under any circumstances.) Nor do you want to give a diamond necklace and get a key chain. (Though this is not as bad as giving the apron.)

When it comes to gift giving, set ground rules. You should both agree to spend X dollars this year. Then stick to it. And only exceed your limit a little.

OffeR to Get a VaseCtomy (anD PRay SHe TaLKS you Out of It)

It makes so much more sense for you to have a little routine procedure than to a) have her insert a diaphragm, b) have her take birth control pills, c) have her get her tubes tied, d) hope you both can count every month better than you balance your checkbook, or e) pray that Mother Nature doesn't have a warped sense of humor. (Of course that condom thing isn't even an option.)

So, offer to have the big V. Snip-snip, it's done. Five minutes. Outpatient. No big deal. Act nonchalant. Cool.

Then leave *National Enquirer* articles around the house about crazed serial killers who masquerade as doctors and leave weird objects (yo-yos, golf tees, an alarm clock) inside patients. Tape and replay the *20/20* specials on surgeons with palsy and nurses who collect body parts. Faint at the sight of blood. Faint at the sight of ketchup. Tell her how much you'd miss her if anything ever happened to you.

Then when she insists you don't get that vasectomy, you can always say, "I offered but you didn't want me to do it."

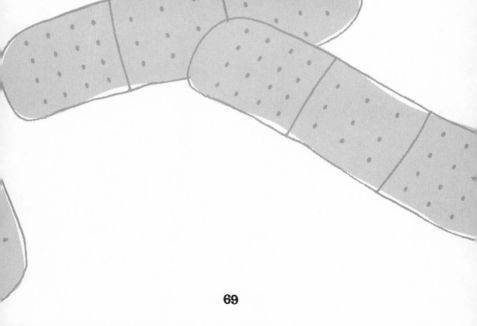

Quit Smoking

Stop today. Right now. Live longer together.

If your wife smokes, this is the one thing you're allowed to pester her to do for you.

Go on a First Date
. . . again

Think of a great place to go. Ask her out. Make reservations. Get dressed up. Shower. Shave. Change socks. Tell her she looks beautiful. Open the car door. Ask for a quiet table. Talk in a low voice. Order wine. Toast her. Share your entrées. Have dessert. Tell her you love her.

You will be her hero for the whole year!

SPenD Time WitHOut OtHeR COuPLeS

Somewhere along the way, social obligations take over your life. You owe this couple or that one. You haven't seen the so-and-sos in so long. You really ought to go out with the you-know-whos because you haven't seen them since who-knows-when.

You get so caught up in going out with other couples, that you forget who you like best: each other.

It's time to go out without anyone else. Just you two. Wow! Isn't your wife cool? And she finds you so fascinating!

BRAG ABOUT YOUR WIFE

Why not? She's probably the best person you know. Tell the world.

TeLL tHe TRUtH

Throughout your relationship, you will be tempted to
hedge, fudge, waffle, wiggle, or just plain lie about things.
But the truth will always come out. Always. Maybe not
today, but tomorrow. Or next week. Or ten years from now.
It will come out. For sure. No doubt. Absolutely. You'll forget
your own story. A friend will let the truth slip. It'll be on CNN.

Just tell the truth in the first place. About everything.
Even if you are just plain wrong. Admit it. Truthfully. Be
honest. About everything. No exceptions. The truth. Always.

Unless she asks if she looks like she's gained weight.

SeX, Money, and Housecleaning are the three Major causes of Marital Friction

everyone knows money is an issue. No couple seems to have enough. So you argue. She spent too much. You didn't spend enough. She didn't earn enough. You didn't save enough. Enough is never enough. (Unless you have too much, which the rich claim is also a problem, but you doubt it.)

And sex can be an issue. When. Where. How. And, of course, enough is never enough.

But the often overlooked fight causer is housecleaning. She thinks you're a pig. You think (but don't say out loud), she's compulsive. You want to be able to sit on the sofa even after she just fluffed the cushions.

She suggests you each make a list of the housecleaning jobs and then divide the combined list equally. You agree. She makes her list. You don't make yours. She takes her list, divides the house in half, gives you all the jobs on your side of the house and takes all those on her side of the house. You agree. She does her half of the jobs. You don't do yours. You say you don't mind if your half of the house is a mess. She does mind. She then cleans your half and says you owe her a cleaning of her half next week. You agree. But you don't do it. She cleans the entire house and dumps everything on your side of the bed. You burrow under it and go to sleep. Eventually mold, mildew, and fungus begin to build up, mice and other field rodents are attracted, buzzards circle your home, and the city condemns your property. For some reason this leads to a fight.

%@$#?!*!

But there is a solution to all three major marital issues—sex, money, and housecleaning. Save up your money. Do not spend it on nonessentials like food or clothing or heat. Instead, hire a maid to come in once a week and clean both halves of the house.

Now, what will you two do with your spare time? Sex.

Get in Sync

Marriages get out of sync. You want to do something but she doesn't. She wants to do something but you don't. The "something" doesn't matter—eating, shopping, reading, cleaning, calling, sitting, standing, mountain climbing— whatever. You're in the mood for X but she's in the mood for Y. Why? Who knows? The two of you are just off-balance. Out of whack, off kilter, out of sorts.

How do you get back in whack, on kilter, or in sorts? Skip a beat. You want to do something but she doesn't. Then don't. She wants to do something but you don't. Then do. Just change the rhythm. What you wanted to do or she wanted to do isn't important. Doing whatever you do together is. (Remember, he who marches to the beat of a different drummer marches all by himself.)

FiGHtS HapPen

You're going to fight. Now matter how well matched, easygoing, or compatible the two of you are, it's inevitable. Soul mates, two halves of the same apple, Jimmy and Rosalyn Carter, George and Martha Washington, Yin and Yang, Ben and Jerry—it happens to every twosome. Even the perfect couple—if there is such a thing—has fights (e.g. "Oh, so you think you're perfect, do you?").

Every husband and wife fight about something some time. She wants to get dressed up and go someplace nice; you want to stay home in your underwear. You like extra-long shag carpeting; she likes bleached hardwood. She wants to get up early and go antiquing; you want to sleep until you become an antique. You say let's rent *Rocky XIII;* she says let's rent *Little Women, the Spinster Years*. You want the Everything Pizza with extra grease; she wants arugula and radicchio salad with no dressing. She says you don't like her friends; you say she's right. You want to watch ESPN Classic

Kickboxing Bouts of the '70s; she wants to read a romance novel with a picture of Fabio on the cover. She says you don't listen to her; you say, "What'd you say?"

She gets upset. You get upset back. Words, louder words, insults, accusations, worse insults, scowls, sulking . . . then long, long, long silences. But there's a good reason.

Fights happen between people who care about each other. People who don't care about each other don't even bother to fight. If your brother-in-law-the-dentist disagrees with the way you raise your child, big deal. What makes him think he's an authority, that starched smock with his name embroidered on the pocket? If the drive-through teller asks who you're voting for and then laughs hysterically, so what? If the package-delivery guy thinks your necktie is ugly, who cares? He wears goofy shorts to work.

But if your wife criticizes your parenting, scoffs at your political views, or thinks your necktie is ugly, it hurts. Because you don't kiss your brother-in-law-the-dentist good-night, hold hands with the drive-through teller, or give an anniversary card to the package-delivery guy. You never asked any of those people to spend their life with you or have your children. You care about your wife and what she thinks. It hurts. It matters. It's supposed to.

Fights are not the end of the world. They don't mean you don't love each other. They mean you do.

Lose

When you do fight, lose. Even if you know you're right. One hundred percent positive. With evidence, eyewitnesses, video cameras, and sworn testimony.

She left the front door unlocked. You locked the front door. You always lock the front door. She has been known, in the past, to forget to lock the front door (and other doors.)

Whoever went out last (your wife) must have left it unlocked.

She's the one who put your home and family in danger.

She says she remembers locking it. But she was definitely the last one out, so . . .

Shut up! The door was left unlocked. So what? Lock it. Go to sleep. Who cares?

And what if you did win the fight? What's the prize? Having your wife annoyed that you proved a stupid point? Is there a trophy commemorating that you proved a stupid point? Can you earn the Olympic gold medal for marital arguing? Is there an electronic scoreboard with a Jumbo-

Tron? Will there be an instant replay of *You-Being-Right?* Will your three-point lead go up in lights? And if there is a scoreboard, are you so sure you won't be behind when the clock runs out?

There's no award for winning fights in marriages. In fact, winning is worse than losing. Lose. Go on with life.

NeVeR aRGUe
aBoUt PoLitiCS

What difference does it make? (Do you think politicians argue about you?)

Don't Stay Mad

What were you so mad about anyway?

MaKe uP

This is the only good part about fighting. One of you apologizes (you). Then you kiss and make up. And whatever else.

The sooner the fight is over, the sooner you make up. So start groveling.

Kiss Good-Night

Make it the one thing you do without exception. Every night. Even if one of you has a fever. Blow each other a kiss. Even if you're out of town. Kiss over the phone. Even if you're in a lousy mood, kiss. You'll be in a better mood.

HaVe CHiLDReN

They're the best thing about getting married. Little people that only you and your wife can make.

Take Pictures

They say everything in memory happens to music. The past is better as a reminiscence than the way it really was. Well, maybe. Or maybe it was really good but you can't appreciate it until you look back.

You and your wife are in this life together. It's your book, your movie, your story. Hold on to it. Take pictures. Save mementos. Keep a scrapbook of life. From time to time, relive your journey. Where you've been. What you've been through. Your first house. The old car that sometimes ran. The kids. The pets. The goofy suit and/or the bad haircut.

This is your life. Enjoy it, appreciate it, laugh, cry, remember. When things get tough, and they will, you can look back at everything you've been through and know you can make it through anything.

LAUGH at NONTRAGIC DISASTERS

Like bounced checks, broken dishes, forgetting to change the oil, losing the remote control, your wife falling asleep during another one of your stories about work/golf/football/high school/this guy you once knew, throwing away your favorite sweatshirt, turning the VCR off before it's finished taping *A Few Good Men,* using your three-wood to kill a bee, her waking you up to ask if you heard a noise.

Laugh because if these things happened to other people, you'd think they were funny. Laugh now because later, when you look back on these things, you'll laugh. Laugh because these things don't matter.

Keep things in perspective.

Unfortunately, there will be plenty of things worth getting upset over.

evolve

Husbands and wives grow during a marriage. Not always in the same ways. Or at the same pace. Careers, promotions, dumb bosses, firings, moves, births, deaths, bills, savings, wrinkles, spare tires, career changes, car accidents, bad phone calls, vacations, operations, graduations, more moves, new ideas, old friends, gray hair, ear hair, no hair, playing the lottery, paying taxes, losing weight, reading a book, having a dream, facing reality, doing something rash/stupid/bold.

Your changes won't be her changes. Hers won't be yours. That's okay. Just don't stand still. Don't get stuck in the past. Keep changing. Keep up with each other. Keep evolving. Remember what happened to the dinosaur.

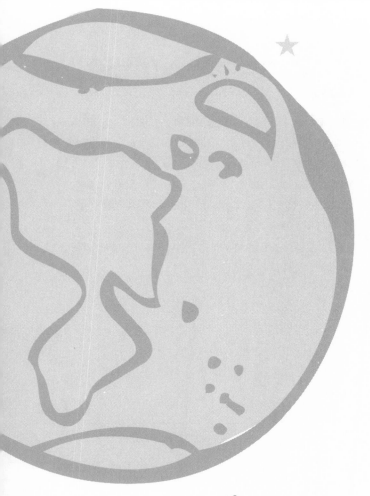

Be a Good Nurse

Despite stereotypes to the contrary, men can be good nurses. When your wife gets sick, you can a) recoil, retch, and act repulsed, b) wear a mask and gloves and keep a safe distance so you don't catch anything, c) have the house doused in antibacterial spray, or d) take care of her every need as she would for you.

So, Floyd Nightengale, you can probably figure out the right answer, can't you?

GROW OLD WITH HER

They say you're only as old as you feel. Well, one day soon, you're going to feel lousy—joints aching, fuzzy eyesight, hard of hearing, and shorter than you were the year before.

Who wants to go through that alone?!

Be an "US," Not a "Me"

Bottom line: The two of you can either be a) you, the husband. And b) her, the wife. Or you can be the two of you. The partnership. The duet. The united front. The team. The force. Be her other half. Let her be yours.

Why be alone? Go us!

Marriage Is Hard Work. Try.

Like many things in life, marriage is work. You're living with someone else. Sharing space, soap, and feelings. You have to understand things you don't really understand (some things have to do with that X and Y chromosome thing). You have to listen, even when you're all listened out. You have to be patient when your fuse is shot. You have to compromise when, more than anything, you want things your way. You have to swallow pride when you couldn't eat another thing. And you even have to admit you're w-r-o-n-g.

But mostly, you have to try. Giving up is easy. Making marriage work is hard. You have to try even when you're really tired, really mad, or know, absolutely, for sure, that you're right (and have photographs and sworn testimony to prove it). You have to try the day after you tried. You have to try for the whole marriage. There's never a day off from trying.

But here's the cool part: It's worth it.

Don't Forget to Have Fun

This is life. Okay, sometimes it's hard. But not always. Sometimes it's fun.

Who are you going to have the good times with? Your wife. She laughs at your jokes more than anyone else. She knows what and who you like and don't like and why. She can interpret your knee-nudges under the table. She can read your eyebrows like Morse code.

She "gets" you. Who else does?